Website
_____

Username
_____

Password
_____

E-mail
_____

Other
_____

Website
_____

Username
_____

Password
_____

E-mail
_____

Other
_____

Website

Username

Password

E-mail

Other

Website

Username

Password

E-mail

Other

Website
_____

Username
_____

Password
_____

E-mail
_____

Other
_____

Website
_____

Username
_____

Password
_____

E-mail
_____

Other
_____

Website

Username

Password

E-mail

Other

Website

Username

Password

E-mail

Other

Website

Username

Password

E-mail

Other

Website

Username

Password

E-mail

Other

Website

Username

Password

E-mail

Other

Website

Username

Password

E-mail

Other

Website

Username

Password

E-mail

Other

Website

Username

Password

E-mail

Other

Website

Username

Password

E-mail

Other

Website

Username

Password

E-mail

Other

Website

Username

Password

E-mail

Other

Website

Username

Password

E-mail

Other

Website

Username

Password

E-mail

Other

Website

Username

Password

E-mail

Other

Website

Username

Password

E-mail

Other

Website

Username

Password

E-mail

Other

Website

Username

Password

E-mail

Other

Website

Username

Password

E-mail

Other

Website

Username

Password

E-mail

Other

Website

Username

Password

E-mail

Other

Website

Username

Password

E-mail

Other

Website

Username

Password

E-mail

Other

Website

Username

Password

E-mail

Other

Website

Username

Password

E-mail

Other

Website

Username

Password

E-mail

Other

Website

Username

Password

E-mail

Other

Website

Username

Password

E-mail

Other

Website

Username

Password

E-mail

Other

Website

Username

Password

E-mail

Other

Website

Username

Password

E-mail

Other

Website
_____

Username
_____

Password
_____

E-mail
_____

Other
_____

Website
_____

Username
_____

Password
_____

E-mail
_____

Other
_____

Website

Username

Password

E-mail

Other

Website

Username

Password

E-mail

Other

Website

Username

Password

E-mail

Other

Website

Username

Password

E-mail

Other

Website

Username

Password

E-mail

Other

Website

Username

Password

E-mail

Other

Website
_____

Username
_____

Password
_____

E-mail
_____

Other
_____

Website
_____

Username
_____

Password
_____

E-mail
_____

Other
_____

Website

Username

Password

E-mail

Other

Website

Username

Password

E-mail

Other

Website

Username

Password

E-mail

Other

Website

Username

Password

E-mail

Other

Website

Username

Password

E-mail

Other

Website

Username

Password

E-mail

Other

Website
_____

Username
_____

Password
_____

E-mail
_____

Other
_____

Website
_____

Username
_____

Password
_____

E-mail
_____

Other
_____

Website

Username

Password

E-mail

Other

Website

Username

Password

E-mail

Other

Website
_____

Username
_____

Password
_____

E-mail
_____

Other
_____

Website
_____

Username
_____

Password
_____

E-mail
_____

Other
_____

Website

Username

Password

E-mail

Other

Website

Username

Password

E-mail

Other

Website

Username

Password

E-mail

Other

Website

Username

Password

E-mail

Other

Website

Username

Password

E-mail

Other

Website

Username

Password

E-mail

Other

Website
_____

Username
_____

Password
_____

E-mail
_____

Other
_____

Website
_____

Username
_____

Password
_____

E-mail
_____

Other
_____

Website
_____

Username
_____

Password
_____

E-mail
_____

Other
_____

Website
_____

Username
_____

Password
_____

E-mail
_____

Other
_____

Website

Username

Password

E-mail

Other

Website

Username

Password

E-mail

Other

Website

Username

Password

E-mail

Other

Website

Username

Password

E-mail

Other

Website
_____

Username
_____

Password
_____

E-mail
_____

Other
_____

Website
_____

Username
_____

Password
_____

E-mail
_____

Other
_____

Website

Username

Password

E-mail

Other

Website

Username

Password

E-mail

Other

Website

Username

Password

E-mail

Other

Website

Username

Password

E-mail

Other

Website

Username

Password

E-mail

Other

Website

Username

Password

E-mail

Other

Website

Username

Password

E-mail

Other

Website

Username

Password

E-mail

Other

Website

Username

Password

E-mail

Other

Website

Username

Password

E-mail

Other

Website
_____

Username
_____

Password
_____

E-mail
_____

Other
_____

Website
_____

Username
_____

Password
_____

E-mail
_____

Other
_____

Website

Username

Password

E-mail

Other

Website

Username

Password

E-mail

Other

Website

Username

Password

E-mail

Other

Website

Username

Password

E-mail

Other

Website
_____

Username
_____

Password
_____

E-mail
_____

Other
_____

Website
_____

Username
_____

Password
_____

E-mail
_____

Other
_____

Website

Username

Password

E-mail

Other

Website

Username

Password

E-mail

Other

Website

Username

Password

E-mail

Other

Website

Username

Password

E-mail

Other

Website

Username

Password

E-mail

Other

Website

Username

Password

E-mail

Other

Website

Username

Password

E-mail

Other

Website

Username

Password

E-mail

Other

<u>Notes</u>